CW00665686

The Islands of Loch Lomond

Clair Calder and Lynn Lindsay

Illustrations by Lynn Lindsay

Northern Books
from Famedram

Printed and published in Scotland by
Famedram Publishers Limited, Formartine, Aberdeenshire.
ISBN: 0 905489 51 9

*"I have seen the Lago di Garda, Albana,
De Vico, Bolsetta and Geneva,and upon my honour,
I prefer Loch Lomond to them all, a preference
which is certainly owing to the verdant islands that
seem to float upon its surface."*

**TOBIAS SMOLLET
1721-1771**

Acknowledgements

WE WISH to thank all those people who so willingly provided information about Loch Lomond's islands. The late Mrs Margaret MacFarlane of Balmaha contributed much from her family's long and celebrated acquaintanceship with the islands and their people. Mrs Scott who owns the house on Inchcruin, Dr and Mrs Cowie of Inchmurrin and Mr and Mrs Scott of Inchmurrin all generously told us about their particular islands, as did Mr MacDonald who until recent times farmed the island of Inchfad. Mrs Claire Moule of Buchanan shared the experience gained from her childhood days on Inchconnachan, while John Cameron and John Mitchell, wardens of the Loch Lomond National Nature Reserve unselfishly gave from their knowledge of the Loch Lomond scene. We also wish to thank C Placido, chief warden with Scottish Natural Heritage, based at Balloch Castle, for information and maps concerning Sites of Special Scientific Interest.

The time-table of the island mail boat and other information was correct at time of writing. However, these details are subject to change from time to time.

Introduction

LOCH LOMOND is situated only 18 miles from Glasgow, making an ideal natural recreation area for the people of Scotland's largest urban conurbation. It can boast of beautiful scenery, consisting of large expanses of water inter-spersed by picturesque and mysterious islands, and all enclosed with a rim of rugged mountains to the north, east and west.

Published statistics regarding the length of the loch vary widely, but the authoritative Bathymetrical Survey of the Scottish FreshWater Lakes, constructed between 1897 and 1907, gives its length as 22.64 miles. It is about 4^1/2 miles wide at its broadest point, and in the narrow northern section reaches the great depth of 105 fathoms or 630 feet. Its surface area of 27^1/2 square miles is the largest of any fresh water lake in Britain.

There has always been controversy over exactly how many islands there are in Loch Lomond, for there are varying definitions of what constitutes an island. Some would include barren rocks while others would say that there must be vegetation. In 800AD Nennius wrote decisively about the number of islands in the Loch.

"The first marvel (of Scotland) is Loch Lomond. In it are sixty islands and men dwell there, and it is surrounded by sixty rocks and an eagle's nest is on every rock; and sixty rivers flow into it, and there issues not therefrom to the sea save one river which is called Leven."

By the eighteenth century Alexander Graham of Duchray gives a slightly more believable report:

"The above ment lake of Loch Lomond is computed to be threttie two miles of watter in length, ...where at its broadest is computed to be about nyne miles of watter. In this Loch are thirtie islands, great and small."

In this book we have included 23 named islands which now form part of Scotland's first National Park.

Access to the Islands

ALL OF the islands of Loch Lomond with the exception of Inchcailloch, Bucinch and Ceardach are privately owned. Inchcailloch belongs to Scottish Natural Heritage, and Buchinch and Ceardach are the property of the National Trust for Scotland. Many of the islands are designated as SSSIs. *(Sites of Special Scientific Interest)*

Access to these three publicly owned islands is freely available to the general public, visiting in small numbers. Prospective visitors to Inchcailloch would be well advised to obtain the excellent booklet about the island, published by Scottish Natural Heritage and written by one of the Loch Lomond Nature Reserve wardens, John Cameron. This gives expert information on Inchcailloch, and can be obtained from the Balmaha boatyard, the Balmaha shop, or from Scottish Natural Heritage. The owners of Inchmurrin welcome visitors to their hotel during its open season, although meals for larger parties and accommodation should be pre-booked.

Whilst most of the owners seem to tolerate responsible use of their beaches by small parties, there are some who actively discourage landing, and as a general rule inhabited areas should be avoided. This includes island piers and jetties which are nearly always private. There are no public toilets on any of the islands.

When islands are visited the Country Code should be conscientiously adhered to. In particular litter should be taken home. The litter problem is ruining the beauty of Loch Lomond, and offenders come from all levels of society. Trees and other plants should not be damaged and in the interests of wildlife, dogs should not be taken to the islands. On Inchmurrin gates should be left shut and fences should not be crossed. In general, keep to foot paths where they exist.

A little care and consideration will help to ensure that the beauty of the islands will remain for all to enjoy.

Contents

Names & their spelling

Old names of islands

OLD NAMES have been taken from maps or in a few cases from texts, dated as indicated. It is evident that in many cases name changes are due to a variety of spellings of the spoken word in an age when spellings were not fixed as they are today, eg: Inche Launak, Inch Lonnag, Inch Lonaig.

In other cases islands have had names quite different from those by which they are known today. Some of these may be due to errors made by map makers in copying from older maps or interpreting imperfectly, information given in a local dialect or in Gaelic.

Spelling of names

THE NAMES in this book are written as on Ordnance Survey, Sheet 56, 1:50,000, 1980. That for example is the only reason why we find Clairinsh instead of Clairinch as we might expect.

Legendary Islands

Camstradden Island

IN CAMSTRADDEN Bay between Inchtavannch and the
mainland are said to be the sunken ruins of the Old
Tower of Camstradden, lost with its orchard beneath the
waters of Loch Lomond at some indefinite time in the
past. In 1868 it was said that when the water level was
low, a pile of stones marking the remains of this island
could be seen under the water. The present mansion of
Camstradden on the mainland was built in 1739, so if
there ever was an island of Camstradden it had
disappeared before this date.

Floating Island

There is a very small island, little more than a gravel
bank, called Floating Island, just off the south-west shore
of Inchconnachan. Perhaps it seems to float when the
water is high and its stunted vegetation moves with the
waves. An old legend of Loch Lomond says that it has
"Waves without wind, fish without fin and a floating
island," and in 1583 it was written that "among the
islands of Loch Lomond is one which floats upon the
water, so that the shepherds who one day have erected
their huts and pens for their sheep on one side of it find
themselves on the morrow on the other side, by the
impetuosity of the winds, which rushing, it is said out of
the caverns of the earth, put the lake into violent
commotion." Such imaginative romancing may have
been based on the rafts of weeds and other vegetation
sometimes dislodged and blown out on to the Loch from
the shallow waters near Luss.

Wee Peter

Wee Peter is not really an island but a statue of a little
boy, set in the water just off Bandry on the mainland and

Legendary Islands

opposite the island of Inchtavannach. Modern day legends have grown up about a boy drowned here and thus remembered, but the truth though less dramatic is kinder. William Kerr was brought up as an orphan in the Village of Luss, and when he grew up he found his way to London where he prospered as a stone mason. The statue, originally made for a London building, lay unused in Kerr's yard for years, until it was brought to Loch Lomond in 1890. Here it was erected some fifty yards offshore to puzzle and stimulate the imaginations of generations of passers by.

L. Lindsay

Crannogs

THESE WERE artificial islands built by Iron Age or even late Bronze Age peoples, as early as the 8th Century BC, for the purposes of security, refuge and defence. Remains of such structures are to be found in lakes throughout the British Isles, and Loch Lomond is no exception. It is thought that Inchgalbraith *(see page 48)* found its origins as a crannog, and another example still showing above the water is Keppinch or The Kitchen *(see page 20)*. Several other crannogs, now usually totally submerged, have been identified in the Loch, perhaps the most notable being that in the bay off Cashel, between Balmaha and Rowardennan on the eastern shore.

From research done on the crannog of Oakbank in Loch Tay by members of the Institute of Maritime Archaeology of the University of St Andrews, we have learned something of how these islets were constructed and used. Heavy wooden piles were driven as much as six feet into the bed of the loch, and large stones were brought, probably on rafts, from the mainland. Many crannogs were approached by a secret, winding, underwater causeway, designed so as to confuse intending intruders, but affording access on foot, albeit with wet feet, to those in the know.

On top of the new island a large, round hut was constructed. Evidence has been found to show that on their crannogs people kept domestic animals, and engaged in everyday economic activities such as spinning wool, and making objects from metal, wood and leather. Nearly always crannog sites are near to good, fertile land on the mainland, from which in all probability the inhabitants gained most of their food and raw materials, returning to the crannog at night or in the face of danger. It is reasonable to assume that life on Loch Lomond crannogs would have been very similar to that on Loch Tay.

Crannogs

Maps of Islands

THE ISLANDS vary widely in size, ranging from the 2.46 kilometre length of Inchmurrin, to tiny Ceardach, with a maxiumum width of 0.04 kilometres. Thus, to make individual island maps to the same scale presents obvious difficulty.

We adopted the solution of varying the scale to accommodate the maps in the space available, and providing a map of the Loch and its islands alongside, as a key to location and a basis for size comparison. The "greatest length" noted in the table of individual maps also gives an indication of size.

Since the book was first published, the Friends of Loch Lomond commissioned a detailed archaeological survey of the islands. This resulted in the publication of three volumes between 1995 and 1998.

Loch Lomond Island Survey – an Archaeological Assessment may be referred to in some of the larger libraries.

ABER ISLE

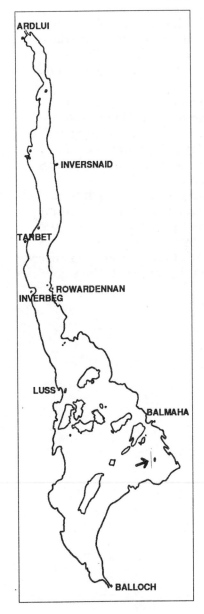

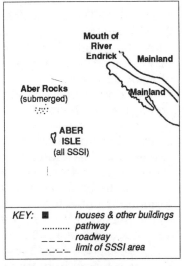

Mouth of
River
Endrick

Mainland

Aber Rocks
(submerged)

Mainland

ꝙ ABER
ISLE
(all SSSI)

KEY: ■   *houses & other buildings*
     .... *pathway*
     _ _ _ _ *roadway*
     _._._._ *limit of SSSI area*

OWNERSHIP – Leased to Scottish Natural
Heritage. Part of Loch Lomond
National Nature Reserve.

OLD NAMES – YI Abbre 1654,
Elan Aber 1745

PARISH – Kilmaronock

POPULATION – Nil

HIGHEST POINT – Just above loch level

GREATEST LENGTH – 0.09 kilometres

FAMOUS VISITORS – St Kessog (?)

BUILDINGS – None

PUBLIC TRANSPORT – None

SSSI – Yes, whole island

'The island at the mouth of the River Endrick'

NEAR TO where the River Endrick flows into Loch Lomond there stood a village called Aber, meaning 'at the mouth of', with a church, a mill and a port from which stone was floated away to the place which was being built into the city of Glasgow. How this community came to an end, probably towards the end of the eighteenth century, is not known, but it left its name to the little island nearby in Loch Lomond.

Situated about half a mile from the mainland and a similar distance south-east of Clairinsh, Aber Isle is little more than a crescent shaped bank of stones, capped by a struggling vegetation of stunted alders, willows and a couple of mysteriously intruding hornbeams. Dominating all is a solitary Scots pine. That it is probably the remnant of a much bigger island when water levels were lower is suggested by a very shallow area of rocks and reefs surrounding it and stretching for some distance towards Clairinsh.

It is unlikely that Aber Isle was ever inhabited, except for temporary purposes of defence or refuge, but perhaps when working nearby during the sixth century, the Irish missionary, St Kessog may have sat his feet on its inhospitable shores. Now part of the Loch Lomond Nature Reserve, Aber Isle comes under the control of Scottish Natural Heritage.

BUCINCH

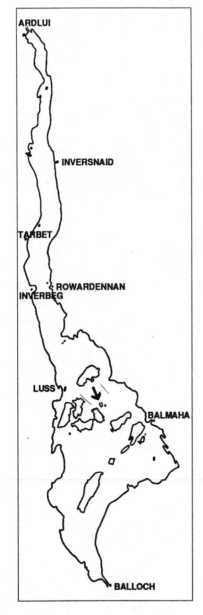

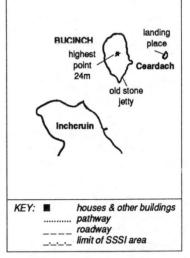

KEY: ■ houses & other buildings
.... pathway
_ _ _ _ roadway
_._._._ limit of SSSI area

OWNERSHIP – National Trust for Scotland
OLD NAMES – YI na Bock 1654, Buckinch 1745
PARISH – Buchanan
POPULATION – Nil
HIGHEST POINT – 24 metres
GREATEST LENGTH – 0.28 kilometres
FAMOUS VISITORS – None recorded
BUILDINGS – Hut Foundations
PUBLIC TRANSPORT – None
SSSI – No

'The island of he-goats'

PERHAPS SOME of the wild, or more accurately, feral goats, still to be found wandering the shores of the Loch under the shadow of Ben Lomond, once lived here, but if so they are long departed. More likely the interpretation of the name is too simplistic and it has other unknown origins. Unlike its near neighbour Inchcruin, Bucinch rises fairly steeply from a rocky coastline to a central summit, but there is no viewpoint as the whole island is clothed in trees. Beautiful, spreading Scots pines cling around its shores, here and there interspersed with birch and rhododendron while inland there is birch and oak and rowan, and almost everywhere a thick carpet of blaeberries. Fixed to a rock on an eastern shore is a little plaque recording the life and death of a young man who must have loved this place.

Gifted to the National Trust for Scotland by Colonel C L Spencer, Bucinch is unrestricted, unsignposted and largely unspoiled. True, its eastern shores are much frequented by campers, some few of whom abuse the privilege of enjoying such surroundings by leaving their garbage behind, but nature helped by clean-up parties succeeds in healing these wounds.

At the southern corner of the island there used to be a small hut for fishermen, the foundations of which are still in evidence, and nearby are the remains of a jetty formed by very large boulders. It is thought that these heavy rocks were brought down from the top of the island on a pulley system, some traces of which may still be seen. Just why a jetty of such massive construction was required here is unknown, although it may have been used for timber extraction.

CEARDACH

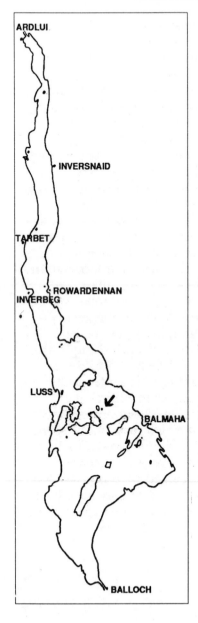

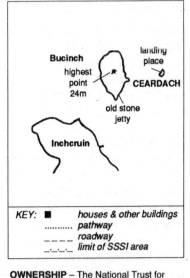

Bucinch

highest
point
24m

landing
place

CEARDACH

old stone
jetty

Inchcruin

ARDLUI

INVERSNAID

TARBET

ROWARDENNAN
INVERBEG

LUSS

BALMAHA

BALLOCH

KEY: ■   houses & other buildings
  ....   pathway
  _ _ _ _   roadway
  _._._   limit of SSSI area

OWNERSHIP – The National Trust for
    Scotland

OLD NAMES – Keardaig 1745,
    Cardag 1777, Cardach 1811, Tinkers
    Island, Gerbil Island

PARISH – Buchanan

POPULATION – Nil

HIGHEST POINT – 10 metres

GREATEST LENGTH – 0.04 kilometres

FAMOUS VISITORS – None recorded

BUILDINGS – None

PUBLIC TRANSPORT – None

SSSI – No

'The smithy'

SITUATED A little to the east of Bucinch and north of Inchcruin, this tiny islet is little more than a rock covered thinly with soil and with fairly deep water all around it. Nevertheless there is an easy landing place for small boats in a natural 'harbour' leading directly on to the gentle sloping area of flat exposed rock, which is a delightful place to lie and take the sun on a summer's day.

Known locally as the *Tinker's Island,* because the Gaelic word *ceard* means both the trade of smith and tinker, experts have found indications that here might have been the site of an Iron Age bloomery or furnace for smelting iron ore. Presumably it was a secure place to work, free from surprise attacks by enemies or wild animals, and supplies of fuel and ore could be transported fairly easily by water. Another more recent name is *Gerbil Island,* because here in the 1960's two gerbils were liberated.

It is amazing how many different varieties of trees and other plants grow on this small rocky place, doubtless originating from seeds brought by birds, by wind and water and occasionally by unsuspecting humans. There is a mature if stunted oak tree, willow, holly, briar and bramble and many other shrubs and smaller plants. During prolonged periods of drought, the thin layer of soil becomes apparent, for trees and plants begin to look distressed, and sometimes the island adopts an autumnal aspect in the height of summer.

Like Bucinch, Ceardach belongs to the National Trust for Scotland.

CLAIRINSH & KEPPINCH

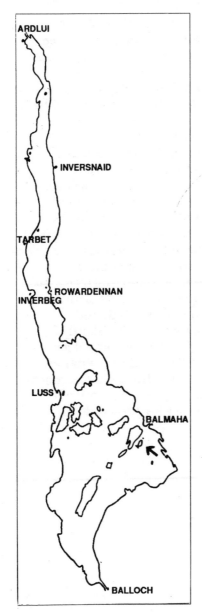

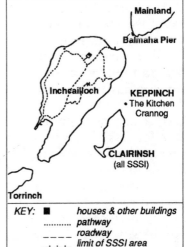

KEY: ■   houses & other buildings
.... pathway
_ _ _ _ roadway
_._._._ limit of SSSI area

OWNERSHIP – Leased to Scottish Natural Heritage. Part of Loch Lomond National Nature Reserve

OLD NAMES – Kuiring 1654, Kuirnig 1725, Clar Inch 1745, Clare Inch 1777, Inch Clear 1811, Clar Innis

PARISH – Buchanan

POPULATION – Nil

HIGHEST POINT – 14 metres

GREATEST LENGTH – 0.46 kilometres

FAMOUS VISITORS – None recorded

BUILDINGS – None

PUBLIC TRANSPORT – None

SSSI – Yes, whole island

'The flat island & the kitchen'

SITUATED JUST east of Inchcailloch, Clairinsh is indeed flat, especially when compared with its almost mountainous neighbour. It is covered in oaks, some old and spreading, and many of them entwined with ivy, and here and there are thickets of holly.

Although small and insignificant looking, Clairinsh has its important place in local history, for in 1225 the Third Earl of Lennox, then owner of much of the southern part of Loch Lomond, granted the island to his clerk. In return the latter, named Buchanan, had to pay a rental of one pound of wax each Christmas! This was the first grant of land to a Buchanan, but the clan grew strong from this small foothold, and until 1682 held sway over much of east Loch Lomond side. Indeed their name lives on in the village of Buchanan near Drymen and the parish of Buchanan stretching from the outskirts of Drymen up the Loch side to Inversnaid. As part of the Barony of Buchanan, Clairinsh was purchased in 1682 by the Third Duke of Montrose, and it remained the property of this family for the next two hundred and fifty years.

However, the Clan Buchanan still looked nostalgically towards this small island which had seen the birth of their grandeur. Indeed over the centuries they had honoured it by using its name as their battle slogan "Clar Innis!" At last, in 1934 they gained possession of Clairinsh once again, when it was acquired for the Buchanan Society. Unlike the long-ago Buchanans who seem to have farmed the island, the new owners took only symbolic occupation, and today Clairinsh is part of the Loch Lomond Nature Reserve, managed by Scottish Natural Heritage.

Just off the northernmost point of Clairinsh lies a tiny man-made island or crannog *(See page 11)*, known as Keppinch or The Kitchen.

CREINCH

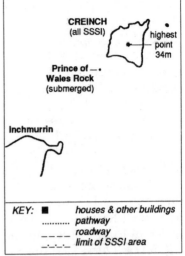

CREINCH
(all SSSI)

highest
point
34m

Prince of —.
Wales Rock
(submerged)

Inchmurrin

KEY: ■   *houses & other buildings*
.... *pathway*
_ _ _ _ *roadway*
_._._._ *limit of SSSI area*

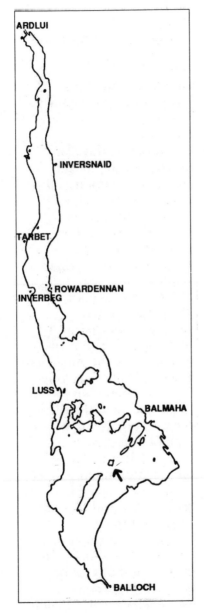

ARDLUI

INVERSNAID

TARBET

ROWARDENNAN
INVERBEG

LUSS

BALMAHA

BALLOCH

OWNERSHIP – Leased to Scottish Natural
Heritage. Part of Loch Lomond
National Nature Reserve

OLD NAMES – Creinche 1654,
Creeinch 1773, Grange 1777,
Inch Croin 1818

PARISH – Kilmaronock

POPULATION – Nil

HIGHEST POINT – 35 metres

GREATEST LENGTH – 0.39 kilometres

FAMOUS VISITORS – None recorded

BUILDINGS – None

PUBLIC TRANSPORT – None

SSSI – Yes, whole island

'The island of trees'

VIEWED FROM the top of the Conic Hill on the mainland above Balmaha, Creinch is seen as the third in a chain of four islands, the others being Inchcailloch, Torrinch and Inchmurrin. These are formed by the high points of a submerged ridge marking the line of the geological Highland fault line. Thus, like the others, Creinch rises steeply from the water to a rounded summit.

As the Gaelic origins of its name implies, it is completely covered in ivy draped trees, including some wych elms, with undergrowth in Summer growing so densely that it can be difficult to penetrate the interior. In Spring it is carpeted in wild garlic, wood hyacinths and wood anemones. But why in a loch rich in forested islands should Creinch be singled out in this way? We must assume that in times gone by when neighbouring islands were farmed and relatively treeless, Creinch was clothed as it is today.

It is an island which guards its secrets well. Its size and position would mark it as a secure refuge for early peoples, harried by enemies or wild animals, but recorded history reveals no evidence of human habitation on Creinch. Now part of Loch Lomond National Nature Reserve, it still preserves its aloofness to man.

EILEAN DEARGANNAN

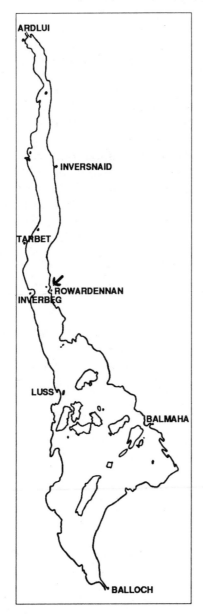

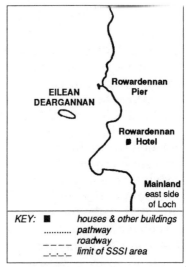

KEY: ■ houses & other buildings
.... pathway
_ _ _ _ roadway
_._._. limit of SSSI area

OWNERSHIP – Private

OLD NAMES – Elan-nan-darragan 1745, Daragan 1773, Ellandergaden 1777, Ellan in Derragha 1818

PARISH – Buchanan

POPULATION – Nil

HIGHEST POINT – Just above loch level

GREATEST LENGTH – 0.11 kilometres

FAMOUS VISITORS – None recorded

BUILDINGS – None

PUBLIC TRANSPORT – None

SSSI – No

'The purple island'

AMONG THE smallest of the islands included in this book, Eilean Deargannan lies not far off Rowardennan pier on the eastern side of the Loch. It is a low stony place covered in willow, alder and some oaks, and is just high enough to stay above the water level for most of the time. There is no record or evidence of any human habitation, although in early times it may well have provided a temporary place of refuge.

A possible derivation of this islet's name is *deargan*, a crimson or purple dye, possibly suggested by a heather clad surface at sometime in the past.

ELLANDERROCH

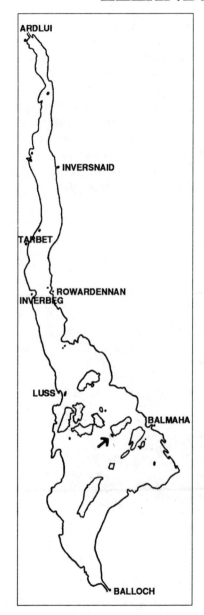

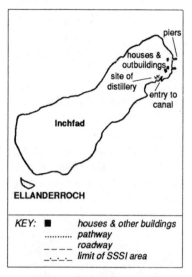

ELLANDERROCH

KEY: ■   *houses & other buildings*
   .... *pathway*
   _ _ _ _ *roadway*
   _._._. *limit of SSSI area*

OWNERSHIP – Private
OLD NAMES – Darrach 1654,
   Ellanderoch 1818
PARISH – Buchanan
POPULATION – Nil
HIGHEST POINT – Just above loch level
GREATEST LENGTH – 0.11 kilometres
FAMOUS VISITORS – None recorded
BUILDINGS – None
PUBLIC TRANSPORT – None
SSSI – No

'The Island of oak'

ONE OF the two islands in the southern or 'lowland' part of the Loch to be named by the Gaelic word *eilean,* meaning island, Ellanderroch is the tiny calf island of Inchfad, being separated from the south-west corner of the latter by about only ten yards of relatively shallow water. When, until recent years, Inchfad was farmed, cattle frequently waded across to the smaller island when the Loch level was low in summer.

For such a small island it has some surprisingly big oak trees including the remains of one preserved by filling its hollow trunk with cement in the 1920s. All that remains of it now is a very charred trunk with a large chunk of masonry inside it, but it serves as a reminder of the dangers to trees on the islands caused by irresponsible fire lighting.

Ellanderroch lies in the centre of an area of the Loch where the fishing is good, and the island is much frequented by anglers who come to eat, rest or take refuge from sudden squalls. Indeed between the wars the Loch Lomond Angling Improvement Association erected an angling shelter on the island, but this has now disappeared without trace.

When one of the former owners of Inchfad sold that island and went to live in England, he retained ownership of Ellanderroch so as to still have 'a bit of Scotland', but the present owners of Inchfad have been able to secure this island as well.

FRAOCH EILEAN

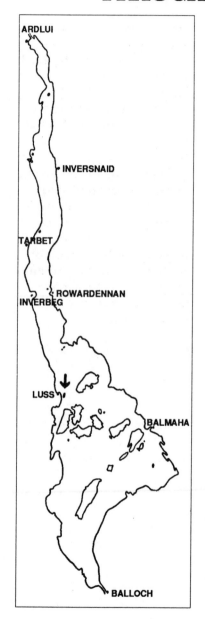

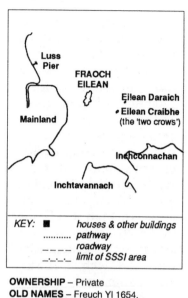

KEY: ■   houses & other buildings
.... pathway
_ _ _ _ roadway
_._._._ limit of SSSI area

OWNERSHIP – Private
OLD NAMES – Freuch YI 1654, Freuchelan 1745, Freuchellan 1773, Inchfrielechan (local, to present)
REGION – Strathclyde
DISTRICT – Dunbarton
PARISH – Luss
POPULATION – Nil
HIGHEST POINT – 15m *(guesstimate)*
GREATEST LENGTH – 0.15 kilometres
FAMOUS VISITORS – None recorded
BUILDINGS – None
PUBLIC TRANSPORT – None
SSSI – No

'The heather island'

JUST OFF Luss on the western shore of the Loch lies this small, long, narrow and very picturesque rocky island. When the heather is in bloom Fraoch is as delightful a rock garden as any made by the hands of man. Now lightly wooded with birches, with, here and there entanglements of brambles, it is said that until the nineteenth century it had many ancient Scots fir trees, but these were destroyed by a disastrous fire which swept the island. Fire must often be a danger to Fraoch, for in dry summers the thin and rocky soils lead quickly to drought conditions, and autumn tints can appear long before their due season. It is surely a paradox that with fathoms of cool, clear water all around them, plants should wither and die for want of it.

It seems that this beautiful place was once inhabited by people who must have been little disposed to appreciate its charms, for on Charles Ross's 1792 *Plan of Dunbartonshire, Loch Lomond and its Environs,* Fraoch is named 'Luss Prison'. Being so near to Luss and yet so isolated and secure, it must have presented a cheap and troublefree solution to the problem of disposal of undesirables. Despite its fair weather delights, it must have been a bleak and inhospitable abode in the teeth of the winter storms. Others too, for lesser crimes, were banished to cool off in this solitude, for we are told it was the place where men of Luss sent 'scolding wives', but whether it had any effect is not revealed!

Fraoch's other name, still used by local people is Inchfrielechan. This is most interesting, because in one name it sems to combine both the Scots and Gaelic words for an island, ie: *Inch-Fraoch-Eilean.* Not far off the eastern shore are two small islands, little more than rocks, known as the Caribidoos or the 'two crows'.

INCHCAILLOCH

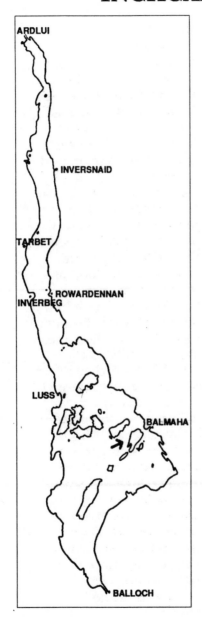

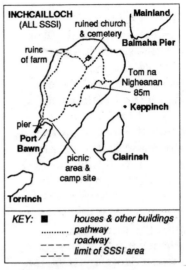

INCHCAILLOCH (ALL SSSI)
ruined church & cemetery
Mainland
Balmaha Pier
ruins of farm
Tom na Nigheanan 85m
Keppinch
pier
Port Bawn
picnic area & camp site
Clairinsh
Torrinch

KEY: ■   houses & other buildings
.... pathway
_ _ _ _ roadway
_._._. limit of SSSI area

ARDLUI

INVERSNAID

TARBET

ROWARDENNAN
INVERBEG

LUSS

BALMAHA

BALLOCH

OWNERSHIP – Scottish Natural Heritage.
Part of Loch Lomond National
Nature Reserve

OLD NAMES – Inche Caille 1654;
Inch Chaille 1725, Inch Caliach 1745,
Inch Calligh 1777, Inch Caillach 1818

PARISH – Buchanan

POPULATION – Nil

HIGHEST POINT – Tom na Nigheanan
85 metres

GREATEST LENGTH – 1.33 kilometres

FAMOUS VISITORS – St Kentigerna

BUILDINGS – Church (ruined),
Farm Buildings (ruined), Hut

PUBLIC TRANSPORT – By arrangement
with McFarlane's Boatyard, Balmaha.
Telephone Balmaha 214. For
permission to use camping area at
Port Bawn, contact the Scottish
Natural Heritage, *Telephone
Alexandria 58511*

SSSI – Yes, whole island

'The island of the old woman or of the nun'

WITH ITS northern end only a few hundred yards from the mainland at the pier of Balmaha, this is one of the most accessible of Loch Lomond's islands. Veiled in oak trees and crowned at its summit by Scots firs, it holds all the mystery of the secret, sacred place which indeed it is.

In 717AD three Christian missionaries arrived in Scotland from Ireland. They were the widowed St Kentigerna, the daughter of a King of Leinster, and her brother and her son. After much travelling the old woman settled on the island, which because of her became known as Inchcailloch. There she died, but her influence endured. It is said that a nunnery was founded, and certainly in the 12th or early 13th century a church was built and dedicated to her memory. To this church for 500 years, from the twelfth to the seventeenth century, the people of the mainland parish, now known as Buchanan and then called Inchcailloch, rowed across to their Sunday worship, and here also they buried their dead. In 1670 the church on Inchcailloch was finally abandoned in favour of one on the mainland, but the graveyard continued to be used into modern times, the last burial being in 1947. Situated on a commanding site about a quarter of a mile above the landing place opposite Balmaha pier, the ancient foundations of the church may still be seen, and many gravestones from more recent times are still legible. Among them is one which witnesses what must be a unique record of a life on Loch Lomond's islands: "Archibald Davie born on Inchfad, 10 March 1839, died on Inchcruin, 12 June 1904". Inchcailloch was the ancient burying place of the Clan MacGregor, but the name most in evidence is MacFarlane. We are indebted to a "gentleman of Dumbarton" for the following account of his attendance of a funeral at

31

INCHCAILLOCH

A corner of the cemetery on Inchcailloch

'The island of the old woman or of the nun'

Inchcailloch towards the end of the eighteenth century:

"I was invited to attend the funeral of a friend from Drymen to Inchcailloch. The funeral party was composed principally of Highlanders, and from the first to the last they had on the journey from sixteen to twenty rounds of the real strong mountain dew, called whisky, which made them so frisky and so inattentive to the solemn business which they had on hand that they very nearly forgot to bury the body."

Among the grave stones are two very old ones to a MacGregor and to a MacFarlane, Gregor MacGregor 1623 and Duncan MacFarlane 1783. The latter bears the clan slogan *Loch Sloy*. Gregor McGregor was chief of his clan and an uncle of Rob Roy MacGregor. According to the Scittish Natural Heritage booklet on Inchcailloch, the table stone was recarved wrongly in the past and should read not 1623 but 1693.

The last permanent inhabitants of Inchcailloch lived there about two hundred years ago, earning their livelihood by farming. The remains of their dwellings can still be traced on the north-west side of the island, near to the shore. The lease of the farm was not renewed after 1770, so it is reasonable to assume that farming was gradually abandoned after this time. Later the land was planted with oak trees, the bark of which was used for the production of leather tanning agents, while the wood was processed to yield pyroligneous acid for use in industry. This processing was done at the 'Liquor Works' on the mainland at Balmaha, in a building which has now been transformed to provide a shop and the *Highland Way Inn*. In the 1920s technical progress made these distillation works redundant, and since then the oak trees have been left to grow,

INCHCAILLOCH

transforming the appearance of Inchcailloch.

Now owned by Scottish Natural Heritage who seek to safeguard the vegetation and wildlife on the island and to encourage natural regeneration, Inchcailloch has become a delight to the many visitors who follow the carefully maintained nature trail wending its circular course from the lowlands to the highlands of this miniature world. Indeed this is not an inaccurate description, as the geological fault line which separates Highland from Lowland Scotland runs longitudinally through Inchcailloch. From the summit viewpoint, surrounded by heather and sheltered by Scots pines, all the major islands of the Loch stretch in beautiful tapestry, to a background of Ben Lomond, Ben Vorlich and the Luss Hills. This is a view which should not be missed! Here, during the Second World War, a low flying Spitfire failed to clear the high trees and crashed, happily leaving the pilot with only a broken leg to worry about. This summit is called Tom na Nigheanan, meaning the hill of the young women, which may have some connection with the nunnery already mentioned.

At the southern end of Inchcailloch is the sheltered, sandy bay known as Port Bawn, probably derived from the Gaelic *ban* meaning white or beautiful. Here Scottish Natural Heritage has provided a wooden jetty and a picnic area, and the shallow, quickly warmed waters of the bay make an enticing place to swim. It is to Port Bawn or to the other wooden pier at the opposite end of the island that visitors must guide their boats, but if they have time to sail a little way away from its shores and view the contours of its dark green length silhouetted against the sky and the water, they can surely see why Inchcailloch was once known locally as 'Corpse Island'.

'The island of the old woman or of the nun'

In *The Lady of the Lake* Sir Walter Scott makes reference to Inchcailloch in his poetic description of the 'fiery cross' sent round by Roderick Dhu to summon the Clan MacGregor to battle. Clan Alpin is another name for the MacGregors.

> *"The shafts and limbs were rods of yew,*
> *Whose fellows in Inch Cailliach wave*
> *Their shadows o'er Clan Alpin's grave,*
> *And, answering Lomond's breezes deep,*
> *Soothe many a chieftain's endless sleep."*

INCHCONNACHAN

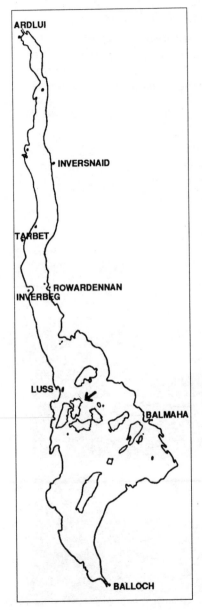

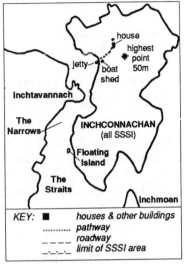

KEY: ■   houses & other buildings
....   pathway
_ _ _ _   roadway
_._._.   limit of SSSI area

OWNERSHIP – Private

OLD NAMES – Inch Connagan 1745, Conagan 1773, Inch Conachan 1777, Inch Conag 1818

PARISH – Luss

POPULATION – Holiday residents

HIGHEST POINT – 50 metres

GREATEST LENGTH – 1.07 kilometres

FAMOUS VISITORS – None recorded

BUILDINGS – House–1, Outbuildings

PUBLIC TRANSPORT – None

SSSI – Yes, whole island

'The Colquhoun's island'

IF ONE could see through its mantle of trees, this would appear a landscape of hill and dale, with few steep gradients or dramatic viewpoints, but with a coastline of secluded, bays that no other of Loch Lomond's islands can excel. All through the summer months these beautiful, secure,tree-fringed havens attract overnighting yachts and cruisers, and day trippers who picnic on their shores. The narrow, winding, river-like strait which separates Inchconnachan from Inchtavannach is the jewel of all the Loch, and we can only agree with the author who early this century wrote: "Whosoever does not know this beautiful strip of water has entirely lived in vain". It is a pity that the peace of these gentle, shallow waters is now all too often destroyed by speeding power boats sometimes towing water skiers, apparantly unaware of the danger and noise pollution caused in such a restricted passage. Writing in the early nineteenth century a local historian observed that although from time to time the Loch southwards of Luss was so frozen "as to allow men with horses and loaded sleds to go from each side to the islands" yet at no time, not even in the great freeze of 1740, did this strait freeze over, despite being nowhere more than 2½ fathoms and having no perceptible current. A trip through *the narrows* as it is popularly known, is a must for anyone exploring Loch Lomond!

Why this particular island of all those belonging to the Colquhouns of Luss should bear a name thought to have been derived from a corruption of their name is not known, especially since of all the Loch's major islands it seems to be the least well documented. Certainly, being so very near to the bridge towards the mainland formed by Inchtavannach, early peoples must have found their way to

37

INCHCONNACHAN

Inchconnachan, and some must have settled here from time to time, but we have little evidence of their occupation. There are some signs that there may have been a settlement towards the north end of the narrows, and a round, well-like structure, possibly a grain drying kiln, has been found. There are also man-made depressions where illicit whisky makers from Luss worked their hidden stills during the last two centuries. It is said that, towards the end of the nineteenth century, a man named Rankine from Luss had the duty of rowing offshore and singing loudly to warn of the approach of revenue men. In the later eighteenth century we are told that the island was all oak and fir wood, and in the mid nineteenth century it is recorded as being uninhabited. Today there is a large wooden bungalow situated near to *the narrows* and snugly wrapped in the forest inland of the wooden pier which serves it. This was until recently the holiday home of Lady Arran, sister of Sir Ivan Colquhoun, formerly the fastest woman on water, having broken her last power boat record at the age of 62. This bungalow was built in the 1920s by a man thought to be a returning eastern tea planter, or retired Admiral, for he was known as Admiral Sulivan. He brought the low wooden verandah architecture of the plantations to this secluded place on Loch Lomond, and lived here with a man-servant until some financial crisis, probably the collapse of the Burmah Oil Company, brought his income and his idyllic lifestyle to an end. Destitute, it is said that he went to live in the dungeon of Island I Vow in the northern part of the Loch. Early in the 1930's the bungalow was bought by William C Buchanan, a Glasgow stockbroker, who for many years commuted from this secret place regardless of the weather, sometimes using a compass to help him find landfall on the mainland. It was he who brought electricity to Inchconnachan, when after his return from war service in 1946 he brought a landing craft powered by two Chrysler engines up the river Leven to transport a generator to the island. He and his family owned and used the house as their main residence until 1970.

On October 16, 1982 the following news item appeared in the *Glasgow Herald*: "Police are investigating a claim by a tanker driver that he collided with a kangaroo about a mile south of Luss on Loch Lomondside. However, while they are sceptical, some people living in the area believe his tale." And well they might believe, for introduced by Lady Arran, wallabies are successfully living wild on Inchconnachan, and it is very possible that one may have made the short journey to the mainland. Walkers wading through the dense scrub and undergrowth of the island are sometimes as startled as the wallaby which bounds up at their feet!

The trees on Inchconnachan are particularly fine, including many beautiful Scots pines, Douglas firs and larch. These have attracted to the island the turkey-like giant grouse of the high tree tops, the magnificent capercaillie. Until the forestry operations in the 1970s reduced the number of trees and thus their food supply of coniferous buds and young shoots, they were here in considerable numbers, their heavy bodies crashing through the high branches in a panicky take-off when disturbed. Although now not so obvious, they may still be seen by the lucky observer. Along *the narrows,* where in Victorian times houseboats lay in quiet seclusion, herons patiently fish among the reeds in the early morning and in the evening, when the clamour of engines is gone and their world reverts to them.

INCHCRUIN

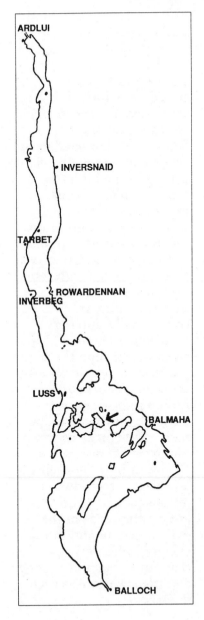

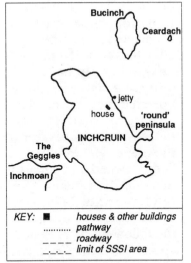

KEY: ■   *houses & other buildings*
    .... *pathway*
    _ _ _ _ *roadway*
    _._._._ *limit of SSSI area*

OWNERSHIP – Private

OLD NAMES – Inch Crowie 1654, Inch Crownig 1725, Chamol 1773, Inch Cruinn 1818

PARISH – Buchanan

POPULATION – Holiday residents

HIGHEST POINT – 20 metres

GREATEST LENGTH – 0.94 kilometres

FAMOUS VISITORS – None recorded

BUILDINGS – Houses : 1, Outbuildings

PUBLIC TRANSPORT – Mail boat from Balmaha, calls if mail when house occupied – no landing

SSSI – No

'The round island'

LOW AND mostly wooded with birch and alder, Inchcruin forms part of the beautiful archipelago in the central part of the Loch. Towards its south-eastern end is a little round peninsula, covered in Scots pines, and joined to the main island by a narrow isthmus, forming sandy bays on both its shores. Elsewhere its coasts are often rock strewn and on the south-west side it all but joins Inchmoan, being separated only by a narrow and shallow strait known to anglers as *The Geggles*.

This may be crossed on foot when the water level is low, and one can imagine the inhabitants of Inchcruin splashing across to Inchmoan in search of their straying cattle. Now the boundary between Central Region and Strathclyde cuts through this strait, as did the old boundary between Stirlingshire and Dunbartonshire.

Why it acquired the name of Inchcruin, which seems to stem from the Gaelic for 'round island' is difficult to appreciate, for it certainly is not round. Perhaps the little round peninsula gave its name to the whole island! Another suggested explanation is that the island may have derived its name from a different Gaelic origin, the expression "chan 'eil e cruinn", meaning 'he is not sane', as in the past it was used for the confinement of insane people.

Belonging to the Montrose estates, Inchcruin was tenanted and farmed certainly into the mid nineteenth century, and probably until much later. The tenants in the early decades of this century seem to have used the island as a holiday retreat, a purpose for which it is still used by the Scott family, the present owners, who maintain the 150 year old cottage sited by the open fields of former arable ground on the eastern shore. Set safely away from the water, dry and snug on a gravel bank, it occupies the site of an

INCHCRUIN

even earlier house, and it has a 1940s extension which originated in the temporary wartime Bellahouston Hospital in Glasgow. The fields have been systematically drained, with tiled channels leading into a main drain, and it is believed that this work was carried out by mentally retarded *inmates* towards the end of the eighteenth century.

Having previously leased the island for rental of about £6 per annum, Mrs Scott's father, Malcolm Irvine bought it from the Montrose Estate in 1930. Mr Irvine worked in the film industry in Glasgow, and during the Second World War he brought many films out to Inchcruin for storage safe from the threat of destruction in air raids. After the war for about eighteen months he became the last person to reside permanently on the island. He kept goats, hens, ducks and geese and grew some small crops, and as there are no springs

he, like his predecessors, had to use the Loch as his water supply. In one respect though his lifestyle was different from theirs, for in a shed behind his cottage he kept his motor lorry, and although there are no roads, he managed to patrol his little kingdom at its wheel!

The lorry was an ex-American Army First World War Dodge, and happily it has survived, restored and cherished by Mr Kerr of Inverbeg.

One day Mr Irvine's billy goat, overcome by loneliness, set out to swim to Inchconnachan, where some of the Buchanan family who resided in the bungalow there, were swimming near the beach. There was consternation when this frightening horned and bearded head was seen cutting through the water towards them and all fled in terror, not knowing that it was only a fellow islander looking for friendship.

'The round island'

Rock on the shore of Inchcruin

43

INCHFAD

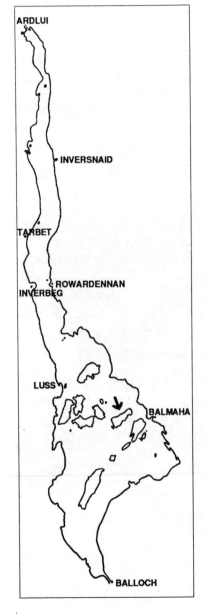

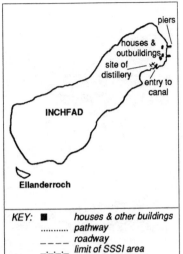

Ellanderroch

OWNERSHIP – Private

OLD NAMES – Inche Fadd 1654, Inch Fado 1773, Inch Fad 1818

PARISH – Buchanan

POPULATION – 2 plus holiday residents

HIGHEST POINT – 24 metres

GREATEST LENGTH – 1.34 kilometres

FAMOUS VISITORS – None recorded

BUILDINGS – Houses 3+, Distillery (ruined)

PUBLIC TRANSPORT – Mail boat from Balmaha – no landing – Calls if mail Monday and Thursday, October to end of April : Monday, Thursday and Saturday, May to end of September *(details Balmaha 214)*

SSSI – No

'The long island'

ISLANDS MADE secure places for illicit whisky distilling, and Loch Lomond's islands are reputed to have been the source of smuggled liquor for the Glasgow market. It was not until the middle of the nineteenth century that a Government revenue cutter sailed the Loch to put an end to this trade. It may have been one of these illicit stills that gained respectability on the island of Inchfad, becoming a registered Government distillery. In any case, by the beginning of the nineteenth century this official distillery was in operation, and its foundations and an old chimney place may be seen today, close to the north-east shore of the island.

The Inchfad distillery was run by Duncan MacFarlane, an ancestor of the MacFarlane family of Balmaha, well known in modern times for their Royal Mail service to Loch Lomond's inhabited islands and for their boatyard at Balmaha. The full barrels were brought by boat to Balmaha, where they were stored until Excisemen supervised their disposal, and presumably most of the grain was imported by water too. On the island a small sheltered canal was dug from the very exposed shore of the Loch right up to the site of the distillery, indicating the importance of water transport in the business. Recently cleared and brought into use as a sheltered harbour by the latest owners of the island, the Inchfad canal is once again serving a useful purpose.

Nearly half a mile in length and lying less than that distance from Balmaha pier, Inchfad is low and green, a meadow-like interior being ringed and sheltered by a deep fringe of alder, birch, ash and some isolated oaks. It has been inhabited and farmed for centuries, and old dry stone walls dividing the fields give evidence of the industry of long gone occupants. Near to the distillery site is the modernised stone cottage

45

INCHFAD

that provided a home for generations of Inchfad farmers, and not far away stands a modern timber bungalow.

For centuries Inchfad belonged to the Montrose family, with their seat at Buchanan on the mainland near Drymen. It was then acquired by the Colonsies of Rowardennan, and under both these ownerships the island was leased out to tenant farmers. It was not until 1944 that it acquired owners who actually lived and tried to earn their livelihood there. These were Ann and Frank Davidson, former aviators, and on Inchfad, pioneering English *white*

House on Inchfad

'The long island'

settlers and forerunners of the *good life* cult. After an abortive attempt to colonise Inchmurrin they bought Inchfad, and over three years made a courageous attempt to support themselves there, mainly by raising Nubian goats and poultry. However the wanderlust was in their blood, and in 1947 they sold Inchfad and set out to sail round the world, an exploit which was to end tragically. Subsequent owners of Inchfad imported caravans and tried to set up a holiday resort, but the island was to return to farming with the coming of Dougie MacDonald, a native of Skye, who knew crofting, and successfully raised beef cattle and sheep on Inchfad until the mid 1980's. After that the island became the private retreat of Ted Toleman, of power boat racing fame, and the area around the houses was landscaped.

Since then it has been sold again and several houses have been constructed near to the distillery site.

The lush green grass of Inchfad attracts Loch Lomond's fallow deer, which may frequently be seen grazing on the fields. The deer are not long term residents, but travel freely between the islands and to the mainland, swimming mainly at dawn or towards dusk in search of new feeding grounds, or perhaps just for the adventure! Another frequent visitor to Inchfad is the wild mink, an illegal immigrant descended from escapees from mink farms.

INCHGALBRAITH

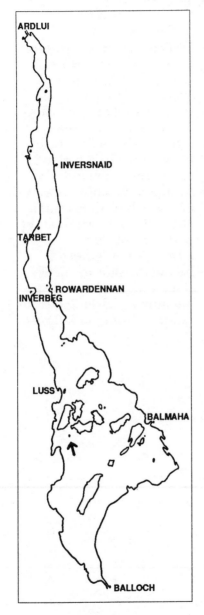

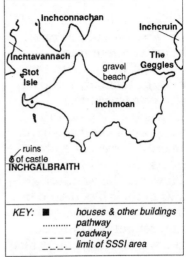

KEY: ■ houses & other buildings
.... pathway
_ _ _ _ roadway
_._._._ limit of SSSI area

OWNERSHIP – Private

OLD NAMES – YI na Castel 1654, Galbroth 1773, Inch Gabreth 1777, Castle Calbreth 1745

PARISH – Luss

POPULATION – Nil

HIGHEST POINT – 9 metres

GREATEST LENGTH – 0.04 kilometres

FAMOUS VISITORS – None recorded

BUILDINGS – Castle (ruined)

PUBLIC TRANSPORT – None

SSSI – No

'The island of the Galbraiths'

THIS TINY islet lying not far south-west of Inchmoan is thought to be a *crannog* or artificial island *(see page 11)*, built by Iron Age people as a dwelling place safe from human and animal predators. There are several other known crannogs in Loch Lomond, the one just off Strathcashell Point on the eastern shore being now merely a heap of stones appearing above the surface when water levels are low – while another is Keppinch or The Kitchen, just off the north of Clairinsh and mentioned on the page given to that island. Usually crannogs could be reached by foot by means of submerged causeways, which followed a circuitous course in order to confuse attackers. Presumably a crannog like Inchgalbraith where the nearest land was an island was doubly secure.

Whatever its primitive man-made origins, the island was found or made strong enough to support the medieval castle of the Galbraiths, the tree camouflaged ruins of which take up most of the island. At one time the Galbraiths owned Bannachra in Glen Fruin, and the erstwhile crannog formed part of this estate. By the beginning of the eighteenth century, and possibly earlier, the castle was already a ruin, and on its topmost point was the eyrie of ospreys, birds which later became extinct throughout the British Isles, but which are now to be seen over Loch Lomond once more. In the last century it was reported that the ospreys on Inchgalbraith had been destroyed by Mr John Colquhoun, author of *The Moor and the Loch,* an act which he was said to have later regretted.

Today, veiled in trees and bushes, the old castle walls still stand high although buffeted by centuries of winter storms, a testimony to the skill of those who built them and to the much earlier men who created the land from which they rise.

INCHLONAIG

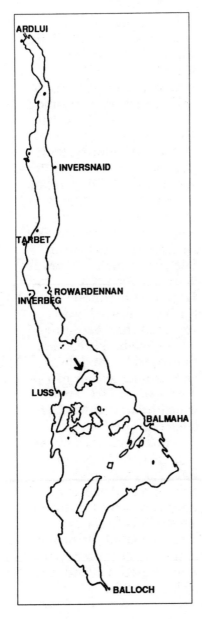

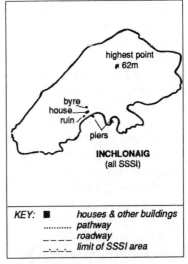

INCHLONAIG
(all SSSI)

KEY: ■   *houses & other buildings*
.... *pathway*
_ _ _ _ *roadway*
_._._._ *limit of SSSI area*

OWNERSHIP – Private

OLD NAMES – Inche Launak 1654,
Inch Paunak 1725, Inch Lonaig 1745,
Inchlonichan 1777, Inch Lonnag 1818

PARISH – Luss

POPULATION – Holiday Residents

HIGHEST POINT – 62 metres

GREATEST LENGTH – 1.60 kilometres

FAMOUS VISITORS – King Robert the
Bruce (?)

BUILDINGS: House : 2 (1 ruined),
Outbuildings

PUBLIC TRANSPORT – None

SSSI – Yes, whole island

'The island of yew trees'

AS ONE approaches the island the dark green of the ancient, gnarled yew trees patterns the hillsides. It is said that they were first planted by King Robert the Bruce in the fourteenth century, to supply bows for his archers. Along with the mainland around Luss, Inchlonaig was granted to the Colquhoun clan by Malcolm, Earl of Lennox in the reign of Alexander the Second, and thereafter for several centuries the Colquhouns used the island as a deer park. A stone built cottage, now used as a holiday home, and the remains of a byre are snugly tucked in just above a bay on the southern shore. Nearby was a large rectangular enclosure, probably used for cultivation. The Admiralty chart of 1861 shows an old limekiln, but this may well have been a kiln for drying grain.

It was in this cottage that a succession of gamekeepers or tenant crofters and their families lived, the last being Angus Colquhoun in the early 1920s. He farmed some of the land, kept two cows, and daily rowed his two daughters to school in Luss. One of his predecessors in the 1830s boarded 'persons that have been addicted to drinking'. Presumably isolation on an island was deemed a certain cure for alcoholism.

In 1873, James Colquhoun of Luss, gamekeepers and a boy, were drowned near Rossdhu after a day's deer shooting on Inchlonaig. Fallow deer, including white deer, may still sometimes be seen on the island.

With its high central ridges and valleys, its many secluded bays and the long vistas through its scattered yew trees, Inchlonaig must be numbered among the most picturesque of the islands. Its hills and dales have long known the footprints of men, for here have been found stone tools which may be as much as 7,000 years old.

INCHMOAN

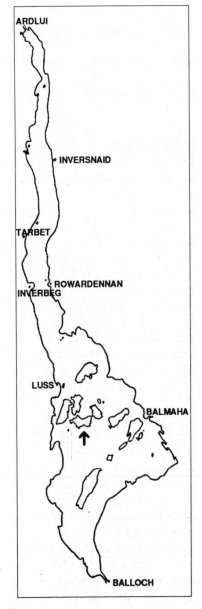

KEY: ■   houses & other buildings
.... pathway
— — — — roadway
_._._._ limit of SSSI area

OWNERSHIP – Private

OLD NAMES – YI na Moin 1654,
Inch Moin 1725, Inch Mone 1818

PARISH – Luss

POPULATION – Nil

HIGHEST POINT – 10 metres

GREATEST LENGTH – 1.41 kilometres

FAMOUS VISITORS – None recorded

BUILDINGS – House–1 (ruined, never completed)

PUBLIC TRANSPORT – None

SSSI – Yes, whole island

'The island of peat'

HERE IS Loch Lomond's Pacific island. There are no shading palms, no coral reefs, but on a summer's day Inchmoan's long, curving sandy beaches become the nearest thing to a tropical paradise that Scotland has to offer. All the activity is on the fringes of the long, flat island for the interior is a jungle of rhododendron, birch, alder, gorse, bog myrtle and blaeberry, the peaceful sanctuary of visiting fallow deer. Only on the western peninsula and at the other extremity of the island, near to Inchcruin, is there a different world of high Scots pines.

Along with Inchlonaig, Inchmoan was granted to the Colquhoun clan by Malcolm, Earl of Lennox, in the reign of Alexander II. Sir Robert Kilpatrick, of Colquhoun, married the daughter of the Laird of Luss, and their descendants became known as the Colquhouns of Luss. Inchmoan has remained the property of the Luss Estate since these far away times. Despite the fact that there are ruins of a substantial building, with wall still standing two storeys high, among the pines on the western peninsula, there is no record of anyone having lived on Inchmoan within historical times. It is said that the ruined building was started by a man from the Vale of Leven early in the nineteenth century, but running out of money he was unable to complete it. Standing gaunt and empty among the pines it conceals its secrets well.

For centuries the mainland inhabitants of Luss used Inchmoan as their source of peat fuel, and in early summer it must have been a hive of industry with boats being rowed out, men cutting deep into the peat banks, and women and children stacking the peats to dry in the summer sun, later to be carried to the boats and brought home in autumn. The narrow shallow strait between Inchmoan and Inchcruin is called 'the Geggles'.

INCHMURRIN

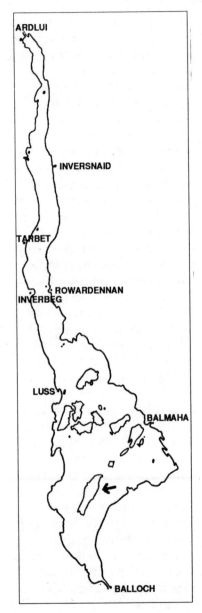

OWNERSHIP – Private

OLD NAMES – Inche Merin 1654, Inchmirin 1745, Inchmerran 1777, Inch Murren 1818.

PARISH – Kilmaronock

POPULATION – 9 plus holiday residents

HIGHEST POINT – Tom Bay, 89 metres

GREATEST LENGTH – 2.46 kilometres

FAMOUS VISITORS – St Mirrin, King Robert the Bruce, King James VI

BUILDINGS – Castle : (1 ruined), Hotel : 1, Houses : 15, Wooden Cabins, Farm Buildings

PUBLIC TRANSPORT: Mail boat from Balmaha gives only short time on the island – Mon & Thurs, October to end of April : Mon, Thurs Sat, May to end of September : Possible increased frequency July & August. *(details from Balmaha 214).* For bar lunches or evening meals *(hotel open Easter to end September)* hotel ferry from Arden by arrangement, *telephone Arden 245.*

SSSI – Yes, north western part of island

'The island of St Mirrin'

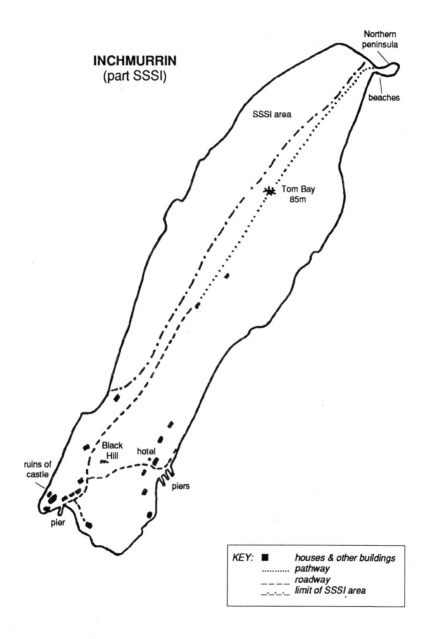

INCHMURRIN
(part SSSI)

Northern
peninsula

beaches

SSSI area

Tom Bay
85m

Black
Hill

hotel

ruins of
castle

piers

pier

KEY: ■ houses & other buildings
.... pathway
_ _ _ _ roadway
_._._._ limit of SSSI area

INCHMURRIN

BY FAR the largest of Loch Lomond's islands, Inchmurrin is truly an enchanting place of woodlands and meadows, high ridge and gentle vale, and always with the water sparkling on all sides. An ideal way to explore it is to sail in to one of the golden gravel bays on the isthmus of the tiny north-east peninsula and from there climb steeply through giant oaks and birches to the open grassy ridge. Leaving plenty of time to linger and enjoy the views from the ridge, descend gradually through vast rhododendron thickets and across rolling meadows to the welcome of the little hotel on the south-east shore. On a bright May morning this little expedition must be among the greatest of pleasures that life can offer.

Set on a headland on the south-westerly extremity of Inchmurrin stand the ruined walls of an ancient castle. It was to this place that the Earl of Lennox with his family and retainers fled in the fourteenth century from his stronghold at Balloch Castle on the mainland, to try to escape from the plague ravaging the neighbourhood. Here also it is believed came Robert the Bruce, later to become victorious King of Scotland, given refuge by the fifth Earl of Lennox after his defeat by the men of Lorne. Inchmurrin Castle too became an exile for the tragic Isabella, Countess of Albany, and daughter of the eighth Earl of Lennox. She had had the nightmare experience of losing her husband, father and two sons, all executed at Stirling on the same day in 1425 at the command of King James I. This terrible toll the King exacted in revenge for his eighteen years of imprisonment in England, an ordeal for which he held the House of Albany responsible. At first imprisoned in Tantallon Castle, she was later allowed to move to what must have been a place of her childhood memories at Inchmurrin, passing her days in religious works until her death in 1460.

Other fragments of Inchmurrin's story have found their way down through the dark mists of time. Sir John Colquhoun of Luss was slain there by the islanders in 1440, but what tale lies behind this dark deed has not been revealed. King James VI of Scotland (and I of England) frequently found his way to the island to enjoy the exhilaration of the deer hunt, and it is said that the notes of the bugle horn often echoed through its woods.

Long, long before all these events, Inchmurrin knew echoes of a gentler kind, as the soft chanting of early Christian monks rose upwards from the chapel they had constructed somewhere towards its southern end. This chapel was dedicated to St Mirrin, and it is likely that he must have visited or even lived here, but in any case his name was given to this peaceful

island. There are places where one can imagine the chapel and its monastic dwellings may have stood, but there is no certain evidence as to its location.

When Inchmurrin Castle fell into disuse and ruin is not known, but along with the other lands of Lennox, Inchmurrin was purchased by the Marquis of Montrose in the seventeenth century, and by 1792 we find the island being described as being well wooded and abounding in pasture and supporting two hundred deer under the care of a gamekeeper and his family working for the Duke of Montrose. About the same time it was written that the people of Inchmurrin belonged to no parish, and it was recommended as 'a place for ladies who had occasion for temporary retirement.'

By the 1830s a 'neat modern cottage for the accommodation of parties of pleasure from the annual residence' had been erected, and fifty years later Inchmurrin was

INCHMURRIN

still the Duke of Montrose's private deer park, inhabited by another in a long succession of gamekeeping families.

Still another fifty years on in 1930, when Inchmurrin was sold by the Montrose Estate to Mr A M Melville, the only habitation was the keeper's lodge, set in a little bay on the short southern shore, where it remains in use today. The new owner had some bungalows built, but soon afterwards the island was sold to the Scott family, who still own it.

The present generation of Scotts, Mr Tom Scott, his wife and sons have worked hard to make Inchmurrin an economic success, and this they have done without spoiling it natural beauty. They run a herd of eighty beef cattle, for which they grow feed of grass and kale. They also own the hotel, opened as a guest house in 1956, and now fully licensed and open from March to October, and for visitors and inhabitants they run a ferry service to the mainland near Arden.

There are now fifteen houses on Inchmurrin, three of which are inhabited permanently, and a cluster of some ten wooden cabins belonging to a naturist club. Much frequented by anglers, watersports people and trippers on the mail boat from Balmaha, Inchmurrin hotel also gets some more exotic visitors, who drop in for dinner by helicopter. If they had the time and patience, they might find the opportunity to get there free and on foot, for very occasionally the southern end of the Loch freezes enough to allow people to walk to and from the mainland. During the great frost of 1895, twenty six thousand people are said to have walked on the Loch on one day, and men of the Montrose Estate transported food and other supplies by horse and cart across the ice to the gamekeeper in the lodge on Inchmurrin.

A great shinty match was played in the vicinity

'The island of St Mirrin'

of the island on a fine sheet of ice, and at the same time skating races and a curling match between married men and single men were taking place further south on the Loch. Many years later, in 1934, another sport brought tragedy when a boat belonging to Loch Lomond Rowing Club was swamped off Inchmurrin and five of the crew were drowned.

In March 1990, when heavy rain and the release of water from hydro-electric dams caused Loch Lomond to rise to the highest levels ever recorded, a house near the southern shore of Inchmurrin had to be temporarily evacuated.

Inchmurrin from the air

L. Linton

59

INCHTAVANNACH

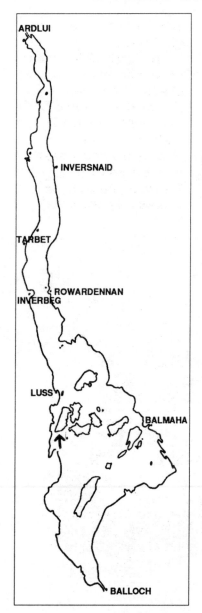

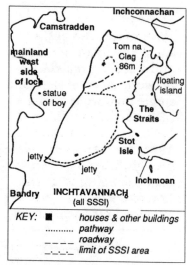

Inchconnachan

Camstradden

mainland
west
side
of loch

• statue
of boy

Tom na
Clag
86m

floating
island

The
Straits

Stot
Isle

jetty

jetty

Inchmoan

Bandry   INCHTAVANNACH
(all SSSI)

KEY: ■   houses & other buildings
.... pathway
_ _ _ _   roadway
_._._._   limit of SSSI area

OWNERSHIP – Private

OLD NAMES – Inche Davannan 1654, Inch Tavannoch 1745, Lavanock 1773, Inch Tavanag 1777, Inch Tannoch 1818

PARISH – Luss

POPULATION – 4

HIGHEST POINT – Tom na Clag 86m

GREATEST LENGTH – 1.47 kilometres

FAMOUS VISITORS – St Kessog, William Wordsworth

BUILDINGS – House–1, Outbuildings

PUBLIC TRANSPORT – Mail boat from Balmaha, calls when there is mail – no landing – Monday and Thursday, October to end of April : Monday, Thursday and Saturday, May to end of September. *Details Balmaha 214*

SSSI – Yes, whole island

ARDLUI

INVERSNAID

TARBET

ROWARDENNAN
INVERBEG

LUSS

BALMAHA

BALLOCH

'The Monk's island'

LYING JUST off the eastern shore of the Loch a little south of Luss, this long wooded island rises abruptly at its northern end to a rocky summit, from which the views to both north and south are among the most beautiful of all Loch Lomond. Here, carved in the flat rock are the initials of long ago ramblers, with dates to show that a hundred years ago people scrambled up to this high viewpoint, just as appreciative of its beauties as are we today. But centuries before them others came too, for this is *Tom-na-clag* – the hill of the bell, where it is said that the monks from a monastery at the southern end of Inchtavannach erected a bell, and tolled it to summon the inhabitants of the parishes of Luss and Inchcailloch to worship.

From near the summit of Tom-na-clag, the traces of what was once a carefully constructed roadway winds down through the birches to a central valley of oaks and a little green meadow on the western shore. Who built this roadway we do not know. It may have been made for the extraction of oak coppice wood in the eighteenth century, but it is pleasant to speculate that perhaps the monks followed its course, and then proceeded across the lower southern part of the island to their monastery, situated where a house and outbuildings now stand. To this place in about the sixth century came St Kessog, bringing Christianity from Ireland, and here he and his followers set up their mission and presumably it was they who first cultivated the long coastal strip which still grows green on the south-east of the island. William Wordsworth must have been thinking of Inchtavannach, which he had visited, when he wrongly referred the following lines to the fortress isle of Island I Vow, much further north.

Within this lonely little isle,
There stood a consecrated pile,

INCHTAVANNACH

Where taper burned and mass
was sung
For those whose timid spirits
clung
To mortal succour, though the
tomb,
Had fix'd, for ever fix'd, their
doom.

St Kessog is believed to have been killed at Bandry Bay just south of Luss and near to the southern tip of Inchtavannach in the sixth century. A large cairn was erected there to his memory and was known as *Cairn-ma-Kessog,* but his effigy which it contained had to be moved to the church of Luss when the cairn was destroyed by soldiers constructing the military road along Loch Lomond during the eighteenth century.

Inchtavannach came into the hands of Alexander Colquhoun of Luss in 1613, and it has remained under the control of the Colquhoun estates since that time. Towards the end of the eighteenth century it was said to have some good pasture and corn fields, and about 1840 it was inhabited by one family, who farmed part of it and boarded out 'persons given to intoxication'. It is reasonable to assume that the substantially built house on the site of the monastery has been continuously inhabited for at least the past two hundred years. It was built in the 1760s and probably replaced a more modest dwelling. The last active tenant farmer was a bachelor called Mr Mc Ewan, who in the 1930s kept cows and grew crops. Since then there has been a succession of tenants using the island primarily as a residence and earning their livelihood elsewhere, and some of these have introduced unusual livestock, such as Jacob's sheep, goats and donkeys, all at some time seen ranging freely on Inchtavannach. Fresh water comes from a mineral spring, which is said to flow from the mainland through a cavity under the Loch.

A recent tenant of the

'The Monk's island'

island was Brian Mahoney, a producer with Scottish Television, who for about ten years enjoyed family life here, and commuted to work in Glasgow. For a time he was producer of *Take the High Road,* based on the nearby village of Luss, a series in which with other Loch Lomond islands, Inchtavannach is frequently seen on the screen. In such a long and close acquaintance with commuting from the island, Mr Mahoney saw most of the varied moods that the Loch can offer, and his short daily voyage to the mainland, usually lasting a few minutes, could take over an hour in the fury of a gale force northerly wind, and once, lost in a fog, he found his trip taking twice that time!

The house on Inchtavannach

INVERUGLAS ISLE

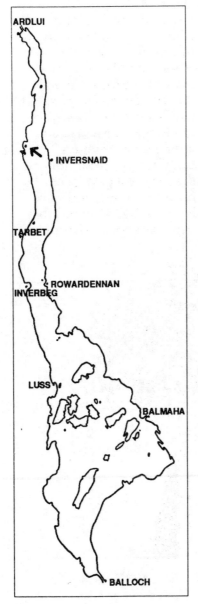

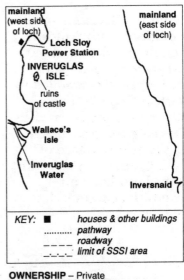

KEY: ■ houses & other buildings
.... pathway
_ _ _ _ roadway
_._._. limit of SSSI area

OWNERSHIP – Private

OLD NAMES – Elan Douglas 1745,
Inveruglas Island 1777

PARISH – Arrochar

POPULATION – Nil

HIGHEST POINT – 10m *(guesstimate)*

GREATEST LENGTH – 0.06 kilometres

FAMOUS VISITORS – None recorded

BUILDINGS – Castle (ruined)

PUBLIC TRANSPORT – None

SSSI – No

'The isle at the mouth of the Black Stream'

THE *BLACK* Stream is the Inveruglas Water which flows from Loch Sloy to enter the Loch just south of the village of Inveruglas on the western shore. This wooded islet lies in the bay just off the village, and should not be confused with Wallace's Isle which is right in the river mouth nearby. Hiding among the high pines near its eastern shore is the ruin of the castle which once was the residence of the chiefs of the Clan MacFarlane and was destroyed by soldiers of Oliver Cromwell during their occupation of Scotland in the seventeenth century.

The MacFarlanes were noted cattle thieves, and the tune played on the bagpipes when the Clan gathered was called 'Lifting the Cattle.' Their battle slogan or war cry was *Loch Sloy*, for in the wild country around this upland Loch, high above Loch Lomond, were their secret fastnesses. In 1543 they raided Garelochside and carried away 280 cattle, 80 sheep, 24 goats, 20 horses, 80 stones of cheese, and 40 bolls of barley, leaving dead any victims who had offered resistance. No doubt some of this booty found its way to the chief's table in the castle of Inveruglas, and one can imagine the feasting and carousing that must have gone on after such a raid.

Among the ruins of the castle, an old sword and keys have been discovered.

ISLAND I VOW

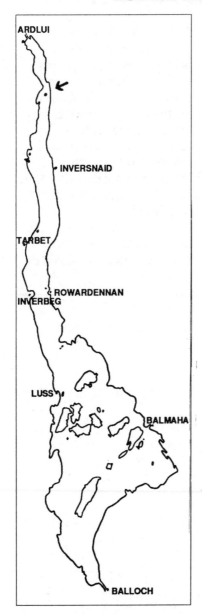

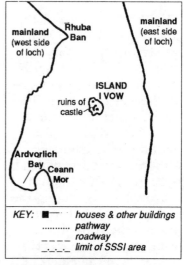

KEY: ■—·· houses & other buildings
.... pathway
_ _ _ _ roadway
_._._._ limit of SSSI area

OWNERSHIP – Private

OLD NAMES – Elan Avero 1745, Avon 1773, Elengavahana 1818 Eilean Vow (local to present)

PARISH – Arrochar

POPULATION – Nil

HIGHEST POINT - 10 metres

GREATEST LENGTH - 0.10 kilometres

FAMOUS VISITORS - William Wordsworth

BUILDINGS – Castle, Outbuildings (ruined)

PUBLIC TRANSPORT - None

SSSI – No

'The island of the cow'

BETTER KNOWN as Eilean Vow, this northernmost of Loch Lomond's islands lies in one of its narrowest parts.

It is a small tree-covered place, but it has had its days of glory, for here the MacFarlanes built their stronghold, after their earlier castle on Inveruglas Isle had been destroyed by Cromwell's troops in the seventeenth century. While the MacGregors were the terror of the eastern shores of the Loch, so the MacFarlanes were the scourge of the western side, and even the moon became known as *MacFarlane's Lantern* because of the aid it gave to them on their midnight cattle rustling raids. It is likely that the name Island I Vow was derived from the Gaelic 'Eilean a' Bho' meaning island of the cow, and that this name owed something to the professional interests of its inhabitants!

The grey ruins of the old castle are still there, shrouded in trees and ivy at the southern end of the islet, and steps still lead down to an arched dank dungeon, which has its own interesting story. In the early eighteenth century the castle was described as "a pretty good house with gardens", but when William Wordsworth visited the island in 1814, it was already a ruin, but an inhabited one. The dungeon had become the home of a hermit, probably an old retainer of the Clan MacFarlane, who somehow managed to exist alone in this isolated place. In his poem *The Brownie's Cell* Wordsworth gave his impressions of the hermit's story:

Proud remnant was he of a
*   fearless race,*
Who stood and flourished face
*   to face*
With their perennial hills...

All were dispossessed, save him
*   whose smile*
Shot lightning through this
*   lonely isle!*
No right had he but what he
*   made*
To this small spot, his leafy
*   shade*

ISLAND I VOW

Seventeen years later Wordsworth returned to Loch Lomond, and hearing that the hermit had been found dead during the intervening years, he penned these lines:

How disappeared he? Ask the newt and toad;
Ask of his fellow men and they will tell
How he was found, cold as an icicle,
Under an arch of that forlorn abode

Castle ruins

'The island of the cow'

It is said that towards
the middle of the present
century during the second
world war, yet another
hermit came and made his
abode on Island I Vow.
Using white stones he laid
out little paths all over the
island, but his tenancy
must have been a relatively
short one, and little is
know of him. It is said that
he may have been the
former tea planter or
Admiral, Sullivan, who
built and lived in the
bungalow on
Inchconnachan, and
having fallen on hard
times found refuge in the
old dungeon here.
Whoever he was, he
paddled his canoe for his
weekly supplies to Ardlui,
and, in the suspicious
climate of the second
world war, was thought by
some to be a German spy!

THE ROSS ISLANDS

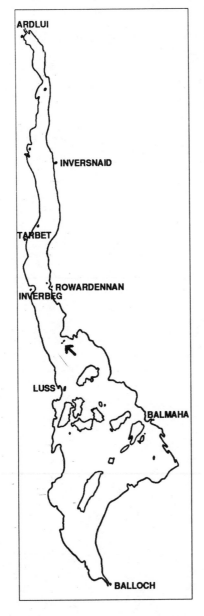

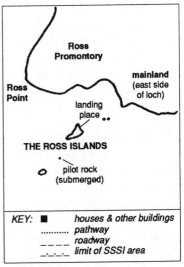

KEY: ■ houses & other buildings
.... pathway
_ _ _ _ roadway
_._._._ limit of SSSI area

OWNERSHIP – Private
OLD NAMES – Ross Inches 1745
PARISH – Buchanan
POPULATION – Nil
HIGHEST POINT – 10 metres
GREATEST LENGTH – 0.09 kilometres
FAMOUS VISITORS – None recorded
BUILDINGS – None
PUBLIC TRANSPORT – None
SSSI – No

70

'The islands off the Ross Promontory'

THESE TWO small islands lie just off the south shore of the great Ross promontory, about two miles south of Rowardennan. Like many of the other smaller islands they are basically rocky ridges appearing above the surface of the Loch, and are lightly vegetated with small trees, mainly birch, holly, rowan and willow, and with heather. The outer and smaller island has no convenient landing place for boats, as the rocky coasts plunge sheer into deep water, while the larger one has a small stony beach on its north-eastern side, and is more varied in its vegetation.

It was while making the passage of these isles in 1850 that The Pilot, one of Loch Lomond's earlier passenger steamers, ran on to a rock, now known as *Pilot Rock,* and had to be steamed on to the beach in order to save herself and her passengers. She was the rival to the Prince Albert operating on the Loch for another company at the same time, and it may have been that competition over time schedules contributed to the accident.

It may be interesting here to comment on the ubiquity of the name *Ross* around Loch Lomond. Besides the Isles, the Point and the Promontory, we find Ross Priory, belonging to the University of Strathclyde, far to the south on the south-eastern shore. Again, almost directly opposite Ross Priory on the western shore we find Rossdhu, the home of the Colquhouns of Luss. In Gaelic 'ros' means a wooded promontory, a name appropriate to all three locations.

71

TARBET ISLE

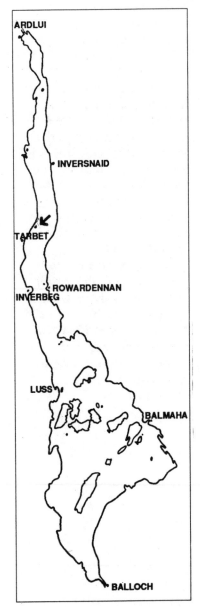

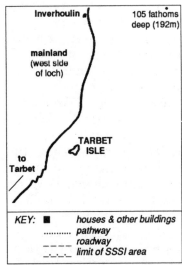

KEY: ■   houses & other buildings
....   pathway
_ _ _ _   roadway
_._._._   limit of SSSI area

OWNERSHIP – Private

OLD NAMES – Elan Tarbet 1745,
Island of Tarbart 1777,
Ellan Tarbet 1818

PARISH – Arrochar

POPULATION – Nil

HIGHEST POINT – 10 metres

GREATEST LENGTH – 0.07 kilometres

FAMOUS VISITORS – None recorded

BUILDINGS – None

PUBLIC TRANSPORT – None

SSSI – No

'The island of the drag boat or portage place'

A VERY small wooded island, with large pine trees and often inhabited with large colonies of gulls, Tarbet takes its name from the nearby village and the isthmus on which it stands. Here the ocean in the shape of Loch Long makes its nearest approach to Loch Lomond, so that the pass from Arrochar to Tarbet made a natural approach for people from the sea wishing access to the land locked Loch. Several other places in Scotland on similar isthmus locations have acquired the same name, notably Tarbert in Argyll, Tarbert on Isle of Gigha, Tarbert on Harris and Tarbet in Morar.

Folklore has it that continuing in the thirteenth century King Haakon's Viking Fleet entered Loch Long, and after dragging their longboats overland across the isthmus, they sailed down Loch Lomond causing alarm and terror to the lochside and island inhabitants. They raided the monastery on Inchtavannach and the church on Inchcailloch, before descending the River Leven to rejoin the ocean via the Firth of Clyde. Is it too much to imagine that they may have used Tarbet Isle as a secure marshalling point before setting out to harry the Loch?

A little north-east of Tarbet Isle and opposite Culness on the eastern shore is the deepest part of the Loch, soundings showing 105 fathoms or 630 feet.

TORRINCH

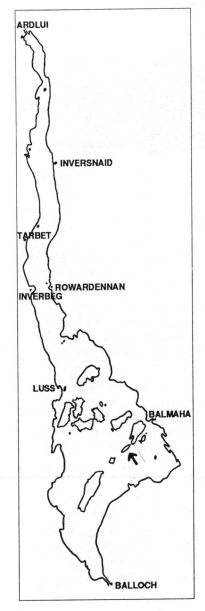

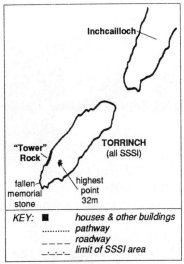

KEY: ■   houses & other buildings
.... pathway
_ _ _ _ roadway
_._._._ limit of SSSI area

OWNERSHIP – Leased to Nature Conservancy Council, Part of Loch Lomond National Nature Reserve

OLD NAMES – Lackow 1654 and 1725, Torinch 1745, Tornish 1777, Torremach 1811

PARISH – Kilmaronock

POPULATION – Nil

HIGHEST POINT – 32 metres

GREATEST LENGTH – 0.64 kilometres

FAMOUS VISITORS – None recorded

BUILDINGS – None

PUBLIC TRANSPORT – None

SSSI – Yes, whole island

'The hill island or the tower island'

THE GAELIC 'tor' meaning a hill, has here been rather appropriately confused with the similar sounding English "tower", but it is in vain that we seek the tower or any remains of it, for so far as can be ascertained, no one ever lived or built anything of great permanence here. The *tower* name is suggested by the sheer face of conglomerate rock which soars one hundred feet

TORRINCH

above the level of the loch at the south-west corner of the island. Seen from afar in the afternoon sun, the rock does assume the aspect of a tower, and the view from the top might well be that from a fortress battlement.

Situated between Creinch and Inchcailloch, Torrinch forms part of the same partly submerged ridge on the fault line. Gently rising from its north-east shore, the greater part of the island is shaded by honeysuckle-garlanded oaks and carpeted by blaeberries and bracken. Towards the south-west it rises abruptly to a little highland place of birches and heather, set at

The fallen monument on Torrinch

'The hill island or the tower island'

the top of the *tower* already mentioned, and nearby is a colony of aspen trees, the leaves of which continuously shake and quiver unless the air is perfectly calm. The old Highland people believed that the aspen trembles because at the Crucifixion the cross was formed from its wood.

In the nineteenth century a disastrous fire swept Torrinch, destroying a forest of Scots fir trees. A few of their descendants still cling to the shoreline, among the oaks, and alders which have stolen their inheritance.

Ignoring the natural bond which unites them, the boundary between Stirling and West Dunbarton cuts through the narrow strait between Torrinch and Inchcailloch, putting Torrinch and the islands on the fault line to the south into West Dunbarton.

On rocks near the island's south-west shore lies a large rectangular piece of hewn stone, a fallen monument to those who perished in a nearby boating tragedy. It is inscribed as follows:

"In memory of Douglas Bryce Wylie Thomas Robertson Carter Clough Ronald Alexander Young David Robert Gilmore lost off Boturich shore during night of 24th May 1908

Erected by their engine works associates and other friends in the employment of John Brown & Co, Clydebank."

WALLACE'S ISLE

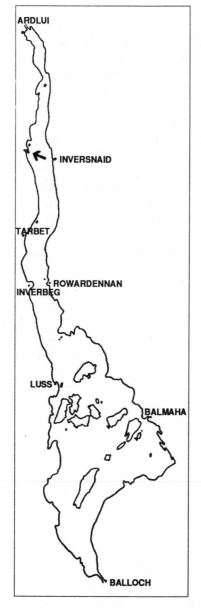

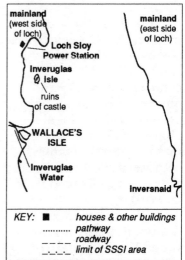

KEY: ■ houses & other buildings
.... pathway
_ _ _ _ roadway
_._._._ limit of SSSI area

OWNERSHIP – Private
OLD NAMES – None recorded
PARISH – Arrochar
POPULATION – Nil
HIGHEST POINT – Just above loch level
GREATEST LENGTH – 0.12 kilometres
FAMOUS VISITORS – None recorded
BUILDINGS – None
PUBLIC TRANSPORT – None
SSSI – No

'The island of someone called Wallace'

LYING LOW and flat and alder covered in the mouth of the Inveruglas Water, just south of the village of Inveruglas, Wallace's Isle has nothing of the beauty or grandeur of most of its fellows. Its claim to fame, is that one of the most famous of Scottish patriots is thought to have taken refuge here. In 1297 Wallace led a rebellion against the English occupation of Scotland, won a great victory at the Battle of Stirling Bridge, drove the enemy out the country and devastated the north of England. Such audacity brought Edward I back to Scotland with a large army and Wallace was defeated. For many years afterwards he carried on a guerrilla war against the English occupiers, often seeking refuge in the mountains. It is known that Wallace operated in the Dumbarton area, so it may have been that he hid from his pursuers on this little island, although it does not now appear to offer much cover or shelter, nor is there any real evidence that he ever came here. A less romantic but perhaps more likely explanation is that the island once belonged to someone else named Wallace. Indeed, in the churchyard of Arrochar there is a gravestone to William Wallace of Inveruglas dated 1814.

Loch Lomond

The verdant islands in this inland sea
of pure fresh water, draw the stranger's eye;
Insh-Murrin's largest... from inclosures free,
Whole flocks of deer in racing haste flee by...
See Duncan Graeme the Forester, where he
Walks with his wife, their dwelling we can spy:
Well, truly they at Kirk and Fair may tell,
That none are furnish'd with a larger well.

Now various islands all at once in sight,
In strange irregularity are seen...
Insh-Torr's thick spreading trees exclude the light;
Insch-Caillaich has a burying ground, between
The shore and yonder trees upon the right...
Insh-Fad's a farm, and wears a lively green...
Isch-Conachan for trusty yews renown'd,
And twenty more are strangely scattered round.

From *Loch Lomond* by William Harriston, 1824